WITHDRAWN
FROM THE RECORDS OF THE
MID-CONTINENT PUBLIC LIBRARY

J973.923 G866
Gresko, Jessica A.
The 1960's

MID-CONTINENT PUBLIC LIBRARY
North Independence Branch
317 W. Highway 24   NI
Independence, MO 64050

AMERICAN HISTORY BY DECADE

The

1960s

Jessica A. Gresko

KIDHAVEN
PRESS™

THOMSON

GALE

San Diego • Detroit • New York • San Francisco • Cleveland
New Haven, Conn. • Waterville, Maine • London • Munich

MID-CONTINENT PUBLIC LIBRARY
North Independence Branch
317 W. Highway 24
Independence, MO 64050
NI

MID-CONTINENT PUBLIC LIBRARY

3 0000 12445974 8

Picture Credits

Cover Photo: © Hulton\Archive by Getty Images
© Bettmann/CORBIS, 8, 13, 18, 33
© Henry Diltz/CORBIS, 26
© Hulton\Archive by Getty Images, 29, 34, 36, 38
Chris Jouan, 14
© Lisa Law, 23, 25, 31, 39
LBJ Library Photo by Yoichi R. Okamoto, 17
Library of Congress, 11
NASA, 5
National Archives and Records Administration, Records of the U.S.
    Marine Corps., 20

© 2004 by KidHaven Press. KidHaven Press is an imprint of The Gale Group, Inc.,
a division of Thomson Learning, Inc.

KidHaven™ and Thomson Learning™ are trademarks used herein under license.

For more information, contact
KidHaven Press
27500 Drake Rd.
Farmington Hills, MI 48331-3535
Or you can visit our Internet site at http://www.gale.com

ALL RIGHTS RESERVED.
No part of this work covered by the copyright hereon may be reproduced or used in any form
or by any means—graphic, electronic, or mechanical, including photocopying, recording,
taping, Web distribution or information storage retrieval systems—without the written
permission of the publisher.

LIBRARY OF CONGRESS CATALOGING-IN-PUBLICATION DATA

Gresko, Jessica A.
  1960s / by Jessica A. Gresko.
    p. cm. — (American history by decade)
Summary: Discusses four major events during the 1960s: the civil rights
movement, the Vietnam War, the emergence of the hippie, and rock music
Includes bibliographical references and index.
  ISBN 0-7377-1748-3 (hardback : alk. paper)
  1. United States—History—1961–1969—Juvenile literature. 2. Nineteen sixties—
Juvenile literature. [1. United States—History—1961-1969. 2. Nineteen sixties.]
I. Title. II. Series.

  E841.G66 2004
  973.923—dc21

                                                    2003001634

Printed in the United States of America

Contents

A Time of Conflict and Change

The 1960s was an era of dizzying change. Nearly every aspect of American life from science and politics to culture underwent a revolution. Some changes happened quickly and peacefully. Others occurred more slowly and, in some cases, painfully.

The conquest of space dominated the decade's science. In 1961 President John F. Kennedy challenged scientists to land a man on the moon. American scientists raced against Russian scientists to see who would be first to reach the moon. In 1969 the world watched on television as American astronaut Neil Armstrong became the first person to walk on the moon. A new era of exploration had been launched. A new frontier, space, had been opened.

In politics, protest was the decade's watchword. Black Americans had long been denied the same rights as other citizens. During the 1960s they protested at lunch counters and bus stations and marched in cities throughout the nation. Their peaceful efforts were often met with violence. Protesters were beaten. Four young black girls were killed when a church was bombed. And then, in 1968, civil rights leader Martin Luther King Jr. was slain in Tennessee.

An American stands on the moon. In 1969, Neil Armstrong and Buzz Aldrin (pictured) became the first people to walk on the moon.

Demonstrators also protested American involvement in Vietnam. During the 1960s, American troops fought Communist forces for control of this Southeast Asian country. As the war dragged on, many Americans at home took to the streets. They waved signs and chanted antiwar slogans. Some young men protested the war by burning their draft cards.

Civil rights and antiwar protests led to many important changes. New laws granted black Americans the same rights enjoyed by other citizens. And public anger over the war eventually ended American involvement in Vietnam.

America was changing culturally, too. Girls and boys began trading their skirts and pressed pants for jeans and T-shirts. Some young people called **hippies** went further. Rejecting the authority of their parents, they grew their hair long and experimented with drugs. Musicians like the popular British group, The Beatles, responded to the changed atmosphere. They created musical styles that reflected the new culture.

From watching the space race on television to dressing in colorful hippie clothing, from marching for civil rights to marching against the Vietnam War, Americans found living in the 1960s an exciting time, sometimes a scary time, a time of conflict and change.

CHAPTER ONE

The Civil Rights Struggle

A t the start of the 1960s America was a segregated country. Especially in the South, black and white citizens lived very separate lives. In the **Deep South** black Americans could not use public libraries or pools. Black children attended overcrowded, run-down schools, and read from outdated textbooks. Signs saying "white" and "colored" told blacks what restrooms and water fountains to use. They sat in separate sections of buses and movie theaters. In many places they were kept from voting. Laws that enforced separation were called Jim Crow laws.

In the 1950s black Americans, and some whites, sought changes. Their actions launched the civil rights movement. In the early 1960s this movement erupted. Black Americans demanded their civil rights, the rights of a citizen to freedom and equal treatment under the law. They made their feelings known by staging sit-ins, freedom rides, and marches.

Sit-Ins Sweep the South

In February 1960 a group of four black college students sat down at a whites-only lunch counter in a Greensboro, North Carolina, store. When they asked to be served, the waitress, who was white, said, "I'm sorry, but we don't serve colored here."[1]

Instead of leaving, the four sat patiently at the counter until the store closed. They left that night but returned the next day with more than a dozen other students. By the end of the week several hundred came to protest.

Soon many more determined students, black and white, were taking part in lunch counter **sit-ins** all across the South. By October 1960 sit-ins had taken place in over one hundred southern cities. Young people did their

Black students participate in a sit-in at a North Carolina lunch counter reserved for white patrons.

homework or wrote letters while waiting at the counters. Sometimes white crowds jeered at them, spat on them, or hit them with purses and clubs. "I was attacked with fists, brass knuckles and the broken portions of glass sugar containers, and was burned with cigarettes . . . covered by salt, sugar, mustard, and various other things,"[2] said John Salter Jr., who participated in a sit-in in Jackson, Mississippi.

The police did little to stop the angry crowds. In many cases they dragged the sit-in participants, not the mobs, to jail. But whether they were jailed or beaten, sit-in participants did not fight back. Like many protests and demonstrations that would follow, sit-ins were nonviolent. In Nashville, Tennessee, for example, when one group was arrested, another simply took its place.

Riding for Equality

Civil rights protests did not stop at lunch counters. Demonstrators also targeted other symbols of segregation like bus stations, where blacks and whites were required to use separate facilities. In 1961 a group of black and white protesters called freedom riders attempted to challenge bus station segregation by riding from Washington, D.C., to New Orleans, Louisiana, trying to integrate the stations along their route.

The first group of thirteen freedom riders boarded buses in Washington, D.C., on May 4, 1961. At rest stops white freedom riders used the bathrooms, waiting rooms, and drinking fountains reserved for "coloreds." Blacks ordered food at white lunch counters and used areas reserved for whites.

At first the freedom riders met little resistance. Though as they rode farther into the Deep South, segregation's stronghold, that changed. In Anniston, Alabama, a waiting mob attacked the freedom riders' bus with chains, sticks,

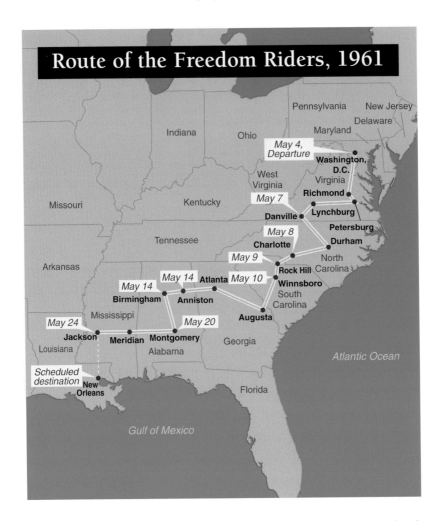

Route of the Freedom Riders, 1961

and iron rods. They broke the windows of the bus, slashed its tires, and pursued it out of town. When the group stopped to fix the tires, the mob firebombed the bus. As the freedom riders fled the burning bus, the crowd attacked them.

A similar mob waited in Birmingham, Alabama, for a second bus. "I could see a mob line up on the sidewalk. . . . Some were carrying ill-concealed iron bars. . . . All had hate showing on their faces,"[3] freedom rider James Peck remembered.

When Peck stepped off the bus, he was beaten. He needed fifty-three stitches to close a bloody wound on his head. Peck and other freedom riders were too badly injured to continue the ride. But newspaper photos of the charred bus and reports of mob brutality had shocked people across the nation. Many decided to help the cause. During the summer of 1961 more than three hundred buses filled with freedom riders traveled through the Deep South to challenge segregation.

The Children's Crusade

As frightening as the violence was, it did not scare off civil rights protesters. Instead, the movement grew. Men and

A Freedom Riders bus spews flames after an attack by an angry white mob.

women of all ages and races participated. But it was a big group of some of the smallest and youngest protesters—children—who were the next to call attention to the struggle. In April 1963 in Birmingham, Alabama, one of the South's most segregated cities, civil rights protesters boycotted stores, picketed, and conducted sit-ins to get the city to desegregate. These demonstrations were not enough. Then children, some as young as six, took to the streets for a march called the Children's Crusade.

Police arrested 959 black children on the first day of the march. Herded onto school buses the children sang freedom songs as they were taken to jail. The next day more than 1,000 children skipped school to continue the march. They did not get far.

The director of public safety, Eugene "Bull" Conner, ordered firemen to turn their powerful hoses on the children to get them to disperse. The water's force ripped the bark off of trees and knocked the children to the ground. Snarling police dogs bit and tore at the marchers, and policemen used clubs and cattle prods to break up the march. Once again the violence and hatred made headlines and was featured on nightly news programs.

The March on Washington

Civil rights marches drew thousands in many different cities. One of the largest marches, called the March on Washington for Jobs and Freedom, took place on August 28, 1963, in Washington, D.C. Organizers expected a big crowd. Spouts were attached to fire hydrants to provide drinking water, and organizers made eighty thousand cheese sandwiches to feed demonstrators. It was not nearly enough. A quarter of a million people marched through the capital's streets. They carried signs with messages like, "No U.S. dough to help Jim Crow grow," "We march for first class citizenship now," and "End segregated rules in public schools."[4]

When they reached the Lincoln Memorial, the sea of people gathered to listen to civil rights leaders speak. Dr. Martin Luther King Jr., one of the best-known civil rights

Civil rights leader Dr. Martin Luther King Jr. waves to the crowd in Washington, D.C., at the end of the 1963 March for Jobs and Freedom.

Then and Now

	1960	2000
U.S. population:	177,830,000	281,421,906
Life expectancy:	Female: 73.1 Male: 66.6	Female: 79.5 Male: 74.1
Average yearly salary:	$4,743	$35,305
Minimum wage:	$1.00 per hour	$5.15 per hour
Unemployment rate:	5.25%	5%

Source: Kingwood College Library.

leaders of the time, spoke last. "I have a dream," he said, "that my four little children will one day live in a nation where they will not be judged by the color of their skin but by the content of their character."[5]

The changes King spoke of were happening—but not fast enough for some people. Frustration turned to violence. Between 1964 and 1967 riots broke out in fifty-eight cities across the country. In Watts, California; Newark, New Jersey; and Detroit, Michigan, rioters smashed store windows, looted, and set fires. More than one hundred people died.

In 1968 Martin Luther King Jr. was assassinated in Tennessee while planning a march. The movement lost an important leader.

Overcoming Obstacles

By the end of the decade the civil rights movement had not solved all the problems facing black Americans, but changes had taken place. Schools, lunch counters, and bus stations were integrated. More black Americans had registered to vote. And tougher laws, including the Civil Rights Act of 1964 and the Voting Rights Act of 1965, made it more difficult to discriminate against black Americans.

Even in Birmingham, Alabama, the mayor repealed all the Jim Crow laws—opening everything from the library to city golf courses to black Americans.

Sit-ins, freedom rides, and marches had been successful. "We shall overcome,"[6] protesters often sang during their demonstrations. By the end of the decade black Americans had overcome a lot.

CHAPTER TWO

Vietnam Divides a Nation

A s the civil rights struggle raged in the United States, a war was beginning in Vietnam, a country in Southeast Asia. American participation in this war began slowly. By the mid-1960s, however, U.S. troops were heavily involved in the fighting.

How It All Started

The origins of the Vietnam War and U.S. involvement are complicated. In 1954 Vietnam won independence from France and was split into two countries. A **Communist** government held power in North Vietnam. A non-Communist government controlled South Vietnam. Soon the Communists and the non-Communists began to fight.

China and the Soviet Union, two Communist countries, helped North Vietnam by sending money and weapons. While not at war, the United States sent aid and military advisers to South Vietnam. American leaders believed communism was a threat to the United States. They also believed that if one country, such as South Vietnam, fell to communism, others would follow. This was called the domino theory.

But war in Vietnam was no game. When Lyndon Johnson became president in November 1963, he felt he had to continue to support South Vietnam. "I am not going to lose in Vietnam,"[7] Johnson said.

In August 1964 Johnson took action. Two American destroyers in the Gulf of Tonkin off the coast of North Vietnam reported being fired upon by the North Vietnamese. Johnson said this was an unprovoked attack and proposed the Gulf of Tonkin Resolution, which Congress passed. It allowed Johnson to send soldiers to fight. The United States was ready for war.

The War Hits Home

At the time the Gulf of Tonkin Resolution was passed, most Americans knew little about Vietnam. To learn what was happening half a world away, Americans turned to television. Nightly, live, and in color, Americans watched the war unfold. From the comfort of their living rooms they saw U.S. soldiers setting fire to a Vietnamese village, murdered women and children, wounded soldiers, and other images of suffering, bloodshed, and destruction. These pictures shocked the nation.

Americans began to take sides. War supporters believed it was their patriotic duty to support the U.S. fight against communism. They held marches where they waved American flags and carried signs that read, "We love America," "Love Our Country," "No Glory Like Old Glory," and

President Lyndon Baines Johnson sent American soldiers to fight in Vietnam.

A Vietnamese family huddles in front of their house as they watch U.S. soldiers enter their village.

"My Country . . . Right or Wrong."[8] Their biggest march in Birmingham, Alabama, in 1969 drew more than one hundred thousand people.

But support for the war faded. As the decade wore on, people who opposed American involvement in the war and wanted U.S. troops brought home held more and more marches and other types of demonstrations.

Dodging the Draft

At first many of the protesters were young men. They knew that they could be called to fight. When a boy turned eighteen he had to register for the **draft** and carry a draft card as proof. But many young men did not want to fight in Vietnam.

Some thought the war was wrong and burned or tore up their draft cards. Others felt their religion prohibited them from killing. Many applied for **conscientious objector** status, which exempted them from fighting. Approximately 170,000 men avoided going to war this way.

Other men tried to dodge the draft by flunking the army's physical exam. They pretended to be crazy, have

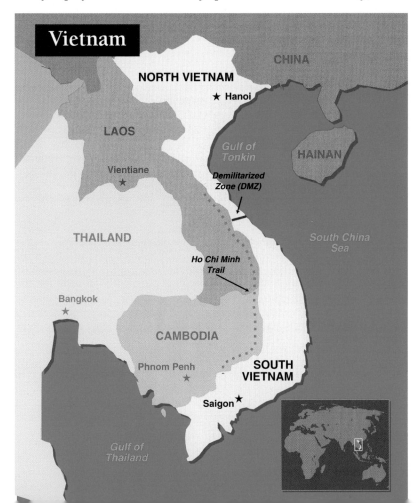

crippling injuries, or be unfit for service in some other way. "For two weeks prior to [the draft physical], I didn't bathe or groom in any way, shape, or form,"[9] said draft resister Gerald Schwartz. He also acted crazy during his physical, swatting at his nose and yelling at the doctor.

As a last resort about 150,000 young men made the hard choice to leave their homes. They fled to countries like Canada and Mexico rather than fight in Vietnam.

A young marine private poses with his gear. Many young men did not want to fight in Vietnam and dodged the draft.

Campus Crusaders

As more young men were called to service, antiwar sentiment spread. Because so many draft-age men were at colleges and universities, numerous protests took place on college campuses. These protests took the form of marches, sit-ins, and **candlelight vigils**.

In March 1965 students and teachers at the University of Michigan at Ann Arbor held a new type of protest. It was called a teach-in. More than three thousand people showed up to hear students, faculty members, and guest speakers explain and debate the war. Other campuses soon followed. Over the next few months teach-ins were held on more than one hundred college campuses across the United States.

Though teach-ins were generally peaceful, sometimes violence erupted during campus protests. In April 1968 Columbia University in New York City was the site of one of the largest student revolts of the decade. Student protesters took over several university buildings and held an administrator hostage. They hoped their actions would convince the university to stop supporting military research.

Protests Pick Up

College students were not the only Americans who opposed the war. Protesters eventually included mothers and fathers, college professors, clergymen, doctors, lawyers, scientists, entertainers, and even congressmen and Vietnam veterans.

Many of the protests this diverse group joined were small and local. But demonstrators also gathered for large marches. More than twenty thousand people marched on Washington, D.C., in 1965. Some were robed in black and wearing skeleton masks. Others chanted slogans such as "Peace now!" and "Hell, no, we won't go!"

In August 1968 ten thousand protesters demonstrated at the Democratic National Convention in Chicago where the party's policy on Vietnam was being decided. These demonstrations spiraled out of control. Protesters taunted policemen. The police fought back with clubs. Soon protesters were throwing anything they could find—from bags of human waste to shoes and chunks of concrete. The Chicago crisis showed protests could become bloody business.

On October 15, 1969, protesters invited the country to participate in a nationwide day of protest called Moratorium Day. In cities across the country, people gathered to listen as the names of soldiers killed in Vietnam were read, to hear speeches, to sign petitions, or to hold candlelight vigils.

The next month, protesters organized a March Against Death in Washington, D.C. For almost two days forty-two thousand demonstrators filed by the White House. Marching single file, each protester carried a candle and a sign with the name of an American who had died in Vietnam. As protesters passed the White House, they called out the name on their sign. The marchers continued on to the Capitol where they placed their signs in coffins.

The Beginning of the End

By this time more than 50 percent of Americans believed U.S. involvement in Vietnam was a mistake. Many of these Americans blamed President Johnson for sending troops to war. At protests they shouted, "Hey, hey, LBJ, how many kids did you kill today?"[10] The war was so unpopular Johnson decided not to run again for president.

The man who succeeded him, Richard Nixon, told the country he had a secret plan to end the war. When Nixon became president in January 1969, he began a program called Vietnamization. This meant that American troops would be pulled out of Vietnam gradually and that Vietnamese soldiers would be responsible for more of the fighting.

Demonstrators in San Francisco gather to protest the war in Vietnam. By late 1969 more than half the country opposed the war.

In the summer of 1969 the first twenty-five thousand American troops left Vietnam. Still, the war dragged on. The last U.S. ground troops did not leave until March 1973.

By that time the war had cost the country $150 billion. More than three hundred thousand Americans had been wounded during the struggle, and more than fifty-eight thousand had lost their lives. The conflict, the longest and most unpopular in the country's history, had divided the nation and left it deeply scarred.

CHAPTER THREE

The Hippie Lifestyle

The rapid changes of the 1960s made teens a very different bunch from their parents. Some teenagers, called hippies, rejected the traditions, goals, and values of the older generation. They formed a culture of their own, a **counterculture**. Its messages were peace, love, and opposition to the Vietnam War.

A Culture of Their Own

Most hippies came from white, middle-class families and were in their late teens or early twenties. Hippies did not value their parents' lifestyles. Their parents worked hard at their jobs in hopes of buying a house and having extra money to spend on vacations, televisions, and other things. Hippies did not care about having good jobs. They did not care about buying a house, buying a television, or taking family vacations.

Hippies also felt society had too many rules. They did not like being told what clothes to wear or how to behave. They wanted more freedom. Just as a group of youths called beatniks had dropped out of society in the 1950s, hippies rejected mainstream values. Some left school and ran away from home.

Many parents did not understand why their hippie children were rebelling, and they felt they could not just ask. The two generations had a hard time talking to one another. One hippie explained, "I can't really communicate to them [my parents] about anything that's really important because they just could not understand it."[11]

Standing in the way of communication was the unique slang used by hippies. To their parents, the words sounded like another language. Hippies used words such as "groovy," "dig," and "far-out." They called guys "cats" and

Hippies ride on top of their colorful bus in a parade. Hippies rejected mainstream values and promoted peace and love.

girls "chicks." Anyone who was not a hippie was referred to as a "square." When they wanted to discuss something they "rapped." When the talk got serious it was "heavy." Their conversations were punctuated with "right on" (I agree) and "out of sight" (terrific).

Far-Out Fashion

Hippies dressed differently, too. At the start of the decade most men and women kept their hair short and well groomed. Boys regularly wore pressed pants and ironed shirts. Girls wore skirts and blouses, or dresses.

A flower child makes a blossom out of paper. Hippies used flowers as symbols of love and peace.

Hippies rejected both of these looks. Hippie men grew bushy beards and mustaches. Both sexes let their hair grow so that it hung down their backs.

Of course, there was not just one hippie look. In general, hippies liked wearing bright colors and wild patterns—batik prints from Indonesia, paisley, and tie-dye. They often found items at thrift stores—including fringed jackets, pieces of military uniforms, bowler hats, American flags, and bandanas—that they put together to create their own style. Jeans went with everything, while footwear ranged from sandals or work boots to no shoes at all.

Hippies also expressed themselves by pinning buttons on everything from vests and jackets to hats. Some buttons made statements like "hippie power," "feelin' groovy," and "flower power." Other buttons expressed political messages: "make love not war," "don't trust anyone over 30," and "you fight & die but can't drink at 18."[12]

Adding to the look, hippies stuck flowers behind their ears. The flowers were thought of as symbols of love and peace. Those who wore flowers, earned the name flower children. Hippies put peace symbols everywhere—on necklaces, earrings, and even painted on their faces. To complete their outfits hippies piled strands of colorful so-called love beads around their necks.

"Turn on, Tune in, and Drop Out"

In addition to being connected with crazy clothing, hippies became associated with drug use. They believed that using drugs, called "tripping out," helped them relax and expand their minds. Some smoked **marijuana**, which put them in a dreamy, calm state. Others took "acid," or **LSD**, a clear, flavorless drug. It produced **hallucinations** that could last for up to twelve hours. "I got very far out, the first time I took it. I had hallucinations . . . for about three hours. I was soaring through time and space,"[13] said former hippie Patrick Gleason, remembering the first time he took the drug.

Bad Trips

But many people who took drugs found they could have nasty side effects. "Bad trips," slang for a bad experience while on a drug, were common. A bad trip on LSD could lead to extreme confusion, panic, depression, or even thoughts of suicide. A person could also be arrested and jailed for illegal use or possession of drugs. Some people who took LSD or marijuana began taking even more dangerous drugs like cocaine and heroin. Despite these risks, many people took drugs anyway.

One man who promoted drug use was onetime Harvard University professor Timothy Leary. Leary believed LSD had many benefits. Leary used LSD himself and believed it awakened a person's spiritual side. He said, "The LSD trip is a religious pilgrimage."[14] He encouraged teens to "turn on, tune in, and drop out," explaining this meant using drugs to learn about oneself and then getting out of mainstream society.

Another pro-LSD figure who helped teens "turn on" was author Ken Kesey. He and a group of followers called the Merry Pranksters hosted giant public parties called Acid Tests. There they treated guests to light shows and music and served LSD in everything from coffee and cake to Pepsi and Kool-Aid.

Drugs even found their way into the music hippies listed to. So-called acid rock songs became popular. These songs described the singers' experiences with drugs and even urged others to try them. Jimi Hendrix, Janis Joplin, The Grateful Dead, Jefferson Airplane, and The Doors became well known for their acid rock songs. For example,

Rock musician Jimi Hendrix performs in concert. The acid rock of musicians like Hendrix was very popular with the hippies.

Jimi Hendrix's "Purple Haze" described the drug experience.

Hippie Hot Spot: San Francisco

The center of hippie happenings was the Haight-Ashbury district of San Francisco, California. At the peak of its popularity, during 1967, about one hundred thousand hippies were living in the area.

They were easy to spot. During the day groups of hippies could be found sitting on sidewalks—**panhandling**, talking, smoking, and playing musical instruments. They spent evenings grooving to colored light shows and music at local dance halls.

In short, the Haight was hippie town. Everywhere signs proclaimed the area's hippie-spirited motto, "Haight is love." The local underground paper, the *Oracle*, was printed in rainbow colors and contained poetry, interviews with people in the hippie community, and information about drugs.

Local stores were owned by hippies and stocked their essentials. The Psychedelic Shop, one of the earliest hippie hangouts, sold beads, bells, feathers, and incense as well as rock records and books about drugs. At Happening House hippies could take classes in yoga or weaving. When they got hungry, twenty-five cents bought a "love burger" at a local restaurant.

Hippies without "bread," slang for money, were given free food and even clothing and medical care by the Diggers, a local hippie theater group that also functioned as a social organization. In fact, sharing was an important part of the hippie spirit. Often a group of hippies shared a cheap apartment or "crash pad." Outside the Haight they might live together in a farmlike setting called a commune, where everyone helped with the chores.

One giant example of hippie togetherness was the World's First Human Be-In. It was held on January 14, 1967 in San

A young man plays guitar in the Haight-Ashbury area of San Francisco, the center of hippie life in the 1960s.

Francisco's Golden Gate Park. Half-picnic, half-party, the "be-in," or gathering, drew twenty thousand people. Stores in the Haight closed for the day so the owners and employees could join the celebration. Flowers, incense, and music were everywhere. Some people brought their own cymbals and tambourines while others listened to music from The Grateful Dead and other bands. The Diggers passed out turkey sandwiches and LSD, and people wandered around enjoying the sunshine and the crowd. The day was a success. Soon, be-ins were taking place across the country.

Though hippies left the Haight at the end of the 1960s, they influenced fashion, music, and language for generations to come.

CHAPTER FOUR

Music Rocks On

When American teens turned on their radios in the 1960s they found the airwaves alive with many different musical styles. There was country music and jazz music, rock and soul, folk music and protest music, California surfer music, and much more.

Rock and Roll

The most popular musical style of the 1960s was rock and roll, later just called rock. Influenced by blues and country music, rock and roll got its start in the 1950s. It was louder and faster than the music before it. And its rebellious nature appealed to teens. Rock-and-roll stars sang about love, fast cars, dancing, and being young. Their tunes were repetitive, easy to remember, and good to sing and dance to.

As some songs were released with their own particular steps, dancing became even more popular. New songs and dances came out every week. To keep up with the newest music fads, many teens tuned in to *American Bandstand*, a television program that showcased rock and roll songs and dances. It featured live singers, dance competitions, and a weekly top ten list. Approximately 20 million enthusiastic fans watched every time it aired. Candice Rich, a regular

American Bandstand viewer, remembered, "I imitated all the dance steps, sometimes with the refrigerator door as a partner. My mother thought I was nuts."[15]

One of the first dances made popular by *American Bandstand* was Chubby Checker's 1960 version of the twist. Unlike earlier dances it could be done without a partner. It was an instant hit.

A group of friends dance the twist. The twist was one of the most popular rock-and-roll dances of the 1960s.

Teens also learned dances like the frug, the monkey, the pony, the mashed potato, and the hully gully. For dances like the swim and the stroll, teens imitated everyday activities.

Adults complained that many teen dances, especially the twist, were indecent. They did not care for all the thrusting and swinging of hips that were part of the dance. Adults also argued that rock music was too loud. Teens did not care. Rock and roll was their music.

Beatlemania

One rock-and-roll band that teens went wild for was a group of four mop-haired singers from England called The Beatles. The Beatles combined American rock and English

John Lennon and Paul McCartney of The Beatles take the stage at a sold-out concert in 1965.

influences in simple love songs. Songs such as "I Want to Hold Your Hand," "I Saw Her Standing There," and "She Loves You" made them an overnight sensation in Britain.

American teens heard The Beatles for the first time on television in 1964. Their performance on *The Ed Sullivan Show* left some of the girls in the audience screaming and crying. Beatlemania had begun.

Soon teens were buying anything associated with The Beatles. Beatle wigs, clothing, dolls, chewing gum, lunch boxes, and even motor scooters flew off store shelves. Sheets and pillowcases the touring group had slept on were cut into three-inch squares. The squares sold for ten dollars each.

Young people copied the way The Beatles wore their hair, the way they dressed, and even the way they talked. Teens stood in long lines to see all four movies The Beatles made and ran to buy every new record. During their first year in America, The Beatles sold more than 2.5 million albums a month. One Beatlemaniac remembered, "My school was in absolute pandemonium. The girls couldn't talk about anything else. . . . We memorized the Beatles' jokes, copied their clothes, and imitated their Liverpudlian slang."[16]

Everywhere The Beatles went, admirers mobbed them. At live concerts screaming fans drowned out the music. A few overwhelmed girls fainted. At a 1966 concert in Cleveland, Ohio, adoring fans climbed onto the stage. Police were sent in to rescue the group.

By the mid- to late- 1960s the group's musical style and message began to change. Their songs reflected the growing counterculture revolution around them, which questioned society's values. As they addressed issues such as the Vietnam War, their lyrics became more serious and meaningful.

Music with a Message

The Beatles were not the only songwriters with a message. Many musicians of the 1960s used their songs to comment

A songwriter and folksinger, Bob Dylan wrote songs with anti-war themes and other strong political messages.

on social changes and political events. Most of the protest music was about peace and Vietnam. Musician Phil Ochs became known for his antiwar tunes like, "Talking Vietnam," "I Ain't Marching Anymore," and "Draft Dodger Rag." Arlo Guthrie's antidraft song, "Alice's Restaurant," became a hit.

The most influential protest songwriter of the decade was gravelly voiced singer Bob Dylan. His songs often had a political message, highlighting problems in society. His song "Blowin' in the Wind" was a powerful antiwar statement and it was often sung at peace rallies. Dylan wrote about the song, "I'm only 21 years old and I know that there's been too many wars. . . . You people over 21 should know better . . . cause after all, you're older and smarter."[17]

Many singers combined music and activism. Singer Joan Baez marched with civil rights leader Martin Luther King Jr. and sang at the 1963 March on Washington. She performed for striking farmworkers in California, protested the death penalty, and was arrested and jailed for antidraft activities. Her actions spoke as loud as the words of her songs.

Woodstock: Three Days of Peace, Music, and Love

Many famous musicians including Joan Baez, Jimi Hendrix, and Janis Joplin came together in August 1969 for a giant outdoor concert. Called the Woodstock Music & Art Fair, it was held on a six-hundred-acre farm in New York.

Organizers expected one hundred thousand people for the three-day festival but many more flocked to the site. Roads leading to the concert were swamped with traffic, backed up for twenty miles. Many young people abandoned their cars and walked. Eventually almost half a million music lovers, many of them hippies, showed up. For that one weekend, the farm became the third largest city in New York.

Organizers had not planned for such a large crowd. They ran short of food, drinking water, toilet paper, and medical supplies. To make matters worse it began to pour. The farm's fields turned to slippery mud.

Instead of becoming angry, people helped each other. They shared food and shelter. People enjoyed sliding in the mud or playing games like tug-of-war. Some cleaned off by going **skinny-dipping**. One concertgoer told a newspaper

The Woodstock Music & Art Fair, advertised in this poster, was a three-day celebration of peace, love, and music.

The band Quill performs at Woodstock to an audience of almost half a million people.

reporter, "I dig it all . . . the mud, the rain, the music, the hassles."[18]

Song and celebration were everywhere. During the day the crowd listened to the music—dancing, clapping, and singing along. There were workshops on playing musical instruments and an arts and crafts fair. At night concertgoers slept in tents or camped out under the stars. Despite the large crowds there was no violence. Even security guards embraced the event's spirit, wearing orange T-shirts with the word *peace* written on the front. To many people the concert symbolized what was best about the Woodstock generation—a spirit of peace and love.

Notes

Chapter One: The Civil Rights Struggle

1. Quoted in Juan Williams, *Eyes on the Prize: America's Civil Rights Years, 1954–1965.* New York: Viking, 1987, p. 127.
2. John R. Salter Jr., "Jackson, Mississippi: An American Chronicle of Struggle and Schism," www.hunterbear.org.
3. Quoted in Peter B. Levy, ed., *Documentary History of the Modern Civil Rights Movement.* New York: Greenwood Press, 1992, p. 78.
4. Library of Congress, "Roy Wilkins with a Few of the 250,000 Participants on the Mall Heading for the Lincoln Memorial in the NAACP March on Washington on August 28, 1963," *Library of Congress Quarterly Journal*, Spring 1982, p. 121, photo.
5. Quoted in Paul Sann, *The Angry Decade: The Sixties.* New York: Crown, 1979, p. 102.
6. Quoted in *Protest Songs in the United States Civil Rights and Antiwar Movement*, www.rede-nonio.min-edu.pt.

Chapter Two: Vietnam Divides a Nation

7. Quoted in Fredrik Logevall, *Choosing War: The Lost Chance for Peace and the Escalation of War in Vietnam.* Berkeley: University of California Press, 1999, p. 77.
8. Quoted in Ezra Bowen, ed., *This Fabulous Century: 1960–1970.* Alexandria, VA: Time-Life Books, 1970, p. 219.
9. Quoted in Sherry Gershon Gottlieb, *Hell No, We Won't Go: Resisting the Draft During the Vietnam War.* New York: Viking, 1991, p. 26.
10. Quoted in Jules Archer, *The Incredible Sixties: The Stormy Years That Changed America.* San Diego: Harcourt Brace Jovanovich, 1986, p. 57.

Chapter Three: The Hippie Lifestyle

11. Speaking in Michael Wadleigh, *Woodstock: Three Days of Music, Peace, and Love. A Once-in-a-Lifetime Celebration*. Burbank, CA: Warner Brothers, 1970, film.
12. Quoted in Bowen, *This Fabulous Century*, p. 31.
13. Quoted in Leonard Wolf, *Voices from the Love Generation*. Boston: Little, Brown, 1968, p. 69.
14. Quoted in Edward P. Morgan, *The 60s Experience: Hard Lessons About Modern America*. Philadelphia: Temple University Press, 1991, p. 197.

Chapter Four: Music Rocks On

15. Candice Rich, "American Bandstand Tidbits," www.fiftiesweb.com.
16. Quoted in Archer, *The Incredible Sixties*, p. 91.
17. Quoted in Robert Shelton, *No Direction Home: The Life and Music of Bob Dylan*. New York: Da Capo Press, 1986, p. 157.
18. Quoted in Josh Mills, "Going Home," in *20th Century America: A Primary Source Collection from the Associated Press*. Vol. 7: Grolier Educational, 1995, p. 113.

Glossary

candlelight vigil: A peaceful gathering usually held at night where participants, carrying candles, sing, chant, or protest silently. During the 1960s candlelight vigils were often held to protest the Vietnam War.

Communist: A person or state that practices or believes in communism, a system of rule in which the government, not private companies or citizens, owns all the land and factories in a country.

conscientious objector: A person whose beliefs or religion prevent him or her from serving in the military. During the Vietnam War if a young man was granted conscientious objector status, he was exempted from fighting but was often required to perform another type of service.

counterculture: A culture, most often made up of young people, that opposes the traditional values and customs of society.

Deep South: The name for a group of some of the most southern states, generally including Georgia, Alabama, Mississippi, and Louisiana. It was in this area that Jim Crow laws and segregation were strictly enforced until the 1960s and where the most intense civil rights protests often took place.

draft: The system of selecting people to serve in the military.

hallucinations: Images that a person imagines seeing but are really created in the mind. Hallucinations can be produced as a side effect of certain drugs like LSD.

hippies: Young people who, during the 1960s, rejected the goals and values of their parents and the older generation. Hippies were also called flower children.

LSD (lysergic acid diethylamide): A clear, flavorless drug that produces hallucinations that can last up to twelve hours.

marijuana: A drug made from the dried leaves and flowers of the hemp plant.

panhandling: Begging for money on the street.

sit-ins: A type of protest used by civil rights demonstrators. During a sit-in protesters would go to a segregated location, most often a lunch counter. They would sit down and often remain until the store closed or they were jailed.

skinny-dipping: Swimming, usually in groups of people, in the nude.

For Further Exploration

Books

Sara Brash and Loretta Britten, eds. *Turbulent Years: The 60s.* Alexandria, VA: Time-Life Books, 1998. Challenging for grade-school readers but well worth the time for excellent, well-organized photos alone.

Stephen Feinstein, *The 1960s: From the Vietnam War to Flower Power.* Berkeley Heights, NJ: Enslow, 2000. Traces the most important issues of the decade including events, lifestyles, politics, and entertainment.

Sally Senzell Isaacs, *America in the Time of Martin Luther King Jr.: The Story of Our Nation from Coast to Coast, from 1948 to 1976.* Chicago: Heinemann Library, 2000. A general illustrated and photographic history broken up into sections.

George Perry, ed., *San Francisco in the Sixties.* London: Pavilion Books, 2001. A photo album of San Francisco in the 1960s that gives the reader a good sense of what the Haight and its inhabitants looked like.

Rose Venable, *The Civil Rights Movement.* Chanhassen, MN: Child's World, 2002. An easy-to-read work that explores the origin and rise of the civil rights movement with photographs and text.

Websites

Civil Rights (www.kodak.com). Black-and-white photographs from the civil rights struggle by photojournalist Charles Moore.

Martin Luther King Jr. (http://seattletimes.nwsource.com). A very manageable website on the civil rights leader with a biography, photo gallery, and time line. The website also contains audio portions and the full text of his famous speeches, including his "I Have a

Dream" speech from the March on Washington in August 1963.

President John F. Kennedy (www.whitehouse.gov). An easy-to-read, one-page biography on Kennedy from the White House website.

President Lyndon B. Johnson (www.lbjlib.utexas.edu). A great site specifically designed for grade-school visitors. Includes audio file interviews with Johnson, a time line, and information specifically about his involvement with the civil rights movement.

Woodstock Music & Art Fair (www.woodstock69. com). Short, guided photo tour through the festival. Also includes lists of performers and the songs they sang.

Index

acid. *See* LSD
American Bandstand (television series),
   32–33
Anniston, Alabama, freedom riders in,
   9–10
antiwar protests, 6, 17–19, 21, 37
   violence and, 21, 22
Armstrong, Neil, 4

Baez, Joan, 37
Beatlemania, 35
Beatles, The, 6, 34–35
beatniks, 24
Birmingham, Alabama
   freedom riders in, 9–10, 12
   Vietnam War protest in, 18
blacks
   civil rights for, 4, 6, 7–15
   discrimination against, 7–15
   protesting by, 7–12

Checker, Chubby, 33
Children's Crusade, 11–12
China, aid to North Vietnam, 16
Civil Rights Act of 1964, 15
civil rights movement
   legislation and, 15
   marches of, 4, 6, 12–14
   protests of, 4, 6, 7–12
   violence and, 9–12, 14
cocaine, 28
Columbia University, student protests
   at, 21
communes, 30
communism, 16
Connor, Eugene "Bull," 12
conscientious objectors, 19
counterculture, 24

dance styles, 33, 34
Democratic National Convention,
   21–22
Detroit, Michigan, riots in, 14
Diggers, 30, 31
domino theory, 16
Doors, The, 28

draft dodging, 19–20
drugs, 27–28, 31
Dylan, Bob, 36–37

Ed Sullivan Show, The (television series),
   35

flower children, 27
freedom riders, 9–11

Gleason, Patrick, 28
Grateful Dead, The, 28, 31
Greensboro, North Carolina, sit-ins in,
   7–8
Gulf of Tonkin Resolution, 17
Guthrie, Arlo, 36

Haight-Ashbury district, 30
Happening House, 30
Hendrix, Jimi, 28–30, 37
heroin, 28
hippies
   drug use and, 6, 27–28
   fashion of, 6, 26–27
   influence of, 31
   language of, 25–28, 30
   symbols of, 27
   values of, 24, 30–31
   Woodstock Festival and, 37–39

integration, 15

Jackson, Mississippi, sit-in in, 9
Jefferson Airplane, 28
Jim Crow laws, 7, 12, 15
Johnson, Lyndon, 16, 22
Joplin, Janis, 28, 37

Kennedy, John F., 4
Kesey, Ken, 28
King, Martin Luther, Jr.
   civil rights march and, 13–14, 37
   death of, 4, 14
   "I have a dream" speech, 13–14

Leary, Timothy, 28

About the Author

Jessica A. Gresko is an award-winning journalist living in New York city. Though her parents were children of the 1960s they claim they were not hippies. This is Ms. Gresko's first book for children.